Electronic Keyboard for Kids

by Sandra Levy & Barbara Siegel

W9-DJI-940

Amsco Publications
New York/London/Sydney

Edited by Amy Appleby
Layout by Mirror Mountain Productions

Order No. AM 70483
US International Standard Book Number: 0.8256.1185.7
UK International Standard Book Number: 0.7119.1447.8

Exclusive Distributors:
Music Sales Corporation
257 Park Avenue South, New York, New York 10010 USA
Music Sales Limited
8/9 Frith Street, London W1V 5TZ England
Music Sales Pty. Limited
120 Rothschild Street, Rosebery, Sydney, NSW 2018, Australia

Printed in the United States of America by
Vicks Lithograph and Printing Corporation

Contents

Foreword

This book is designed for children ages seven to twelve that have electronic keyboards with automatic chords and rhythm. Its purpose is to teach them to read music, and to use the different automatic features of the electronic keyboard. *Electronic Keyboard for Kids* also teaches basic music skills, such as finger coordination, playing notes on the treble and bass staves, and the understanding and use of rhythm. It will help the young student acquire the ability to play a standard piece of piano music through practice of simple exercises and familiar children's songs. The child will also learn to read a lead sheet (or chord chart), so commonly used by popular musicians today.

Electronic Keyboard for Kids will explore the different automatic functions of the keyboard, such as single and fingered chords, automatic rhythm, and synchro start, as well as special effects such as fill-in, variation, and duet. When this course has been completed, the student will have a basic knowledge of music, and will be prepared to learn more complicated functions that will enable him or her to move easily to the study of other keyboard instruments, such as piano, synthesizer, or organ.

Preparing to Play

If you walk up to a piano and press down any key, you will hear a sound. If you have an electronic keyboard, there are things you need to do before you can make it play a sound.

First you need to turn the power on. If you use batteries, be careful not to let them get worn out, as this will affect the sounds your keyboard makes.

You can make your keyboard sound like different instruments in a band or orchestra. These sounds are called *Registrations.* You will find a guide at the beginning of each song. One of the things that it will tell you is what Registration to use. If your keyboard does not have the sound that the guide calls for, you may choose another sound that is similar, or one that sounds good to you.

Your keyboard has a *Rhythm* section. Turn this on by pressing the *Start,* or *Start/Stop* control on your keyboard. The guide at the beginning of each song will also tell you what rhythm to use. If it says *Off,* this means you won't be using the Rhythm section. If you do not have the rhythm that the guide calls for, try to pick a similar rhythm that will be easy for you to play with.

Another thing that the guide tells you is how to set your *Auto Chord* section. This is also sometimes called the *Auto Bass Chord,* or *Accompaniment* section. The guide for each song will tell you whether you will be using *Single Finger* or *Fingered* chords. If the guide says *Off,* don't turn the chord section on. This way, you will be playing your electronic keyboard just like you would a piano.

Make sure you always read the guide at the beginning of each song, and any other instructions that might be written out for you, very carefully. This will make playing your electronic keyboard much easier. Remember, always read your owner's manual if you have any questions about your keyboard.

Position at the Keyboard

Make sure your keyboard is on a stand or a table before you sit at the keyboard.

Your feet should touch the floor.
Your knees should be right under the keyboard.
Sit up very straight and tall.

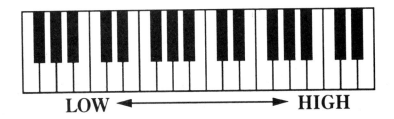

A keyboard is divided into white and black keys. The *black keys* are divided into groups of two and three.

Turn on your keyboard. SET the Registration to *Piano* for this exercise.

PLAY all the groups of two black keys up and down the keyboard.

PLAY all the groups of three black keys up and down the keyboard.

Do you hear the difference between the high and low notes?

Your Fingers

WIGGLE each finger as you SAY its number:

1 for your **thumb**
2 for your **pointer finger**
3 for your **middle finger**
4 for your **ring finger**
5 for your **pinky**

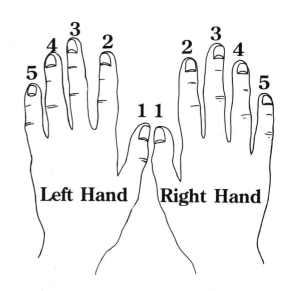

Left Hand   Right Hand

Introduction to Rhythm

Music has long sounds and short sounds. When we put them together, we call this *rhythm*. A *quarter note* lasts for one count. A *half note* lasts for two counts. This is how they look when they are written.

Quarter Note   **Half Note**

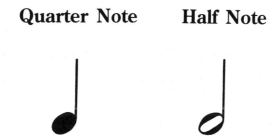

Notes are divided into groups. These groups are separated into *measures*. The lines that divide the measures are called *bar lines*. A *double bar line* marks the end of a song.

SAY and CLAP this rhythm. SAY "quarter" when you come to a quarter note, and "half-note" when you come to a half note.

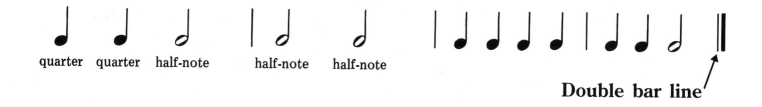

quarter   quarter   half-note   half-note   half-note

Double bar line

We're Ready to Play

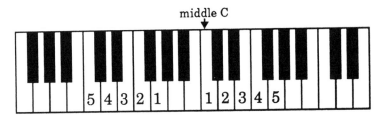

middle C

Left Hand   Right Hand

PLACE your fingers on the keyboard, as shown above.
CURVE your fingers.
WATCH your music, not your fingers!
PLAY each song and SAY the finger numbers aloud.

Registration: Piano
Rhythm: Off
Auto Chord: Off

Right Hand

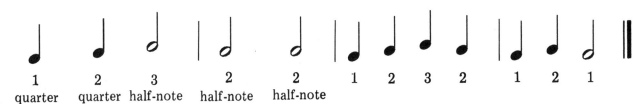

Registration: Piano
Rhythm: Off
Auto Chord: Off

Left Hand

Now PLAY each song again and COUNT the rhythm by saying
"quarter" or "half-note," as we did before.

Another kind of music note looks like this:

O
Whole Note

This is called a *whole note.* To count its rhythm let's say: "great-big-whole-note."

SAY and CLAP this rhythm. When you come to the *repeat sign* at the end of this song, go back to the beginning of the song and SAY and CLAP it out one more time.

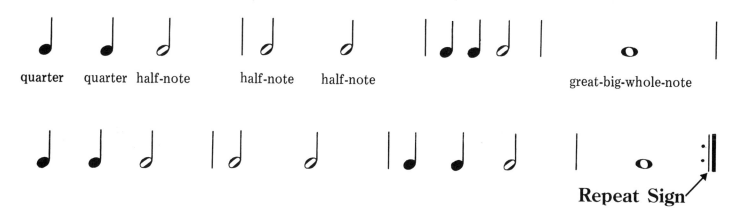

quarter   quarter   half-note   half-note   half-note   great-big-whole-note

Repeat Sign

Now let's try another song.
PLAY this song with your *right hand.*
FIND the keyboard position again.
SAY the finger numbers aloud as you play.

Registration: Piano
Rhythm: Off
Auto Chord: Off

Right Hand

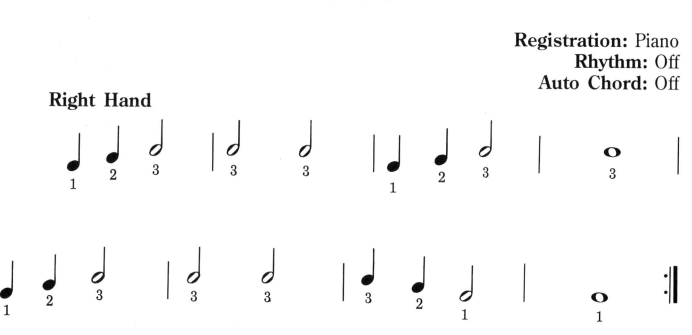

PLAY the song again and COUNT the rhythm as you play.
REMEMBER, the repeat sign means you should go right back to the beginning and play it once again.

SAY and CLAP this rhythm.

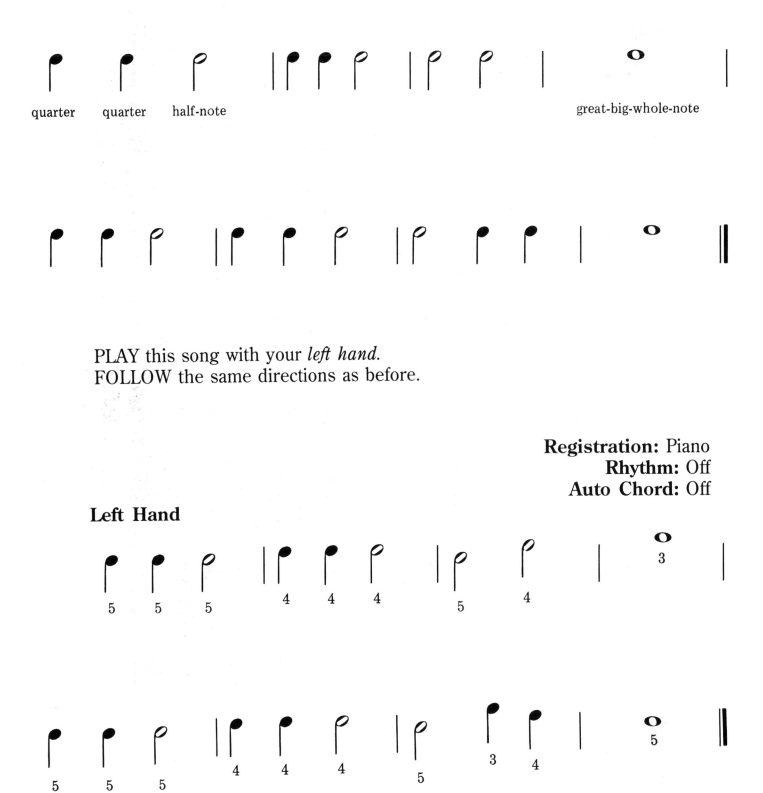

PLAY this song with your *left hand.*
FOLLOW the same directions as before.

Registration: Piano
Rhythm: Off
Auto Chord: Off

Left Hand

Introduction to the Musical Alphabet

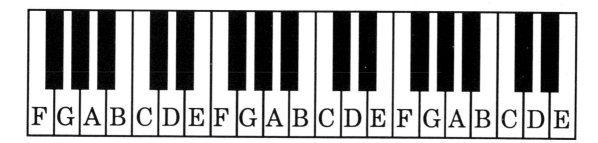

There are only seven letters in the musical alphabet. These letters name the *white keys*. Remember that the black keys come in groups of twos and threes. These groups of black keys will help you find the white keys.

The note named C is always to the left of every group of two black keys.
The note named F is always to the left of every group of three black keys.
FIND all the C's and F's on your keyboard.

Now that you know where C is, D and E are right next door!

Now FIND F again. G, A, and B are right after that!

Now PLAY and SAY each note and its letter up and down the keyboard.
Start with the C's.
The D's are next door.
The E's are after that.
Then play all the F's, G's, A's, and B's.

Now let's put it all together. Start at the lowest note of your keyboard. PLAY and SAY each note and its letter going up.

When you come down, the alphabet goes backwards. SAY the alphabet backwards as you PLAY each note down the keyboard.

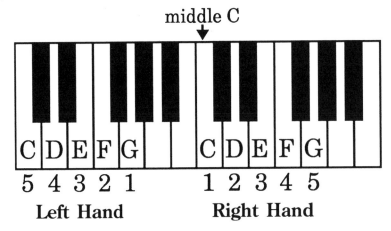

PLACE both hands on your keyboard, as shown in the picture above.
Remember to CURVE your fingers.
WATCH your music–not your hands.

PLAY this song and SAY the finger numbers.
PLAY the song again and SAY the note names aloud as you play.

Registration: Piano
Rhythm: Off
Auto Chord: Off

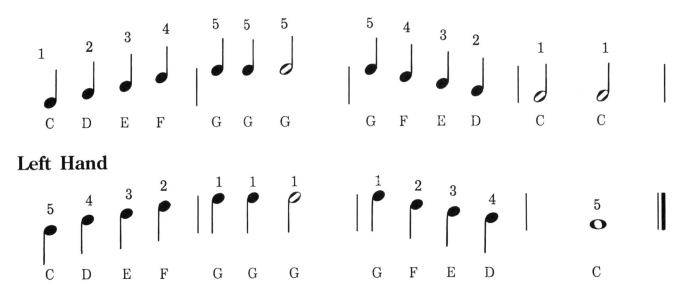

GO BACK once more and COUNT the rhythm of the notes aloud.

How Notes Move

When you go from one note to the very next note, it is called *stepping*. You can step up and down the keyboard, just like stepping up and down stairs.

PLAY this next song and follow the same directions as before.

Registration: Piano
Rhythm: Off
Auto Chord: Off

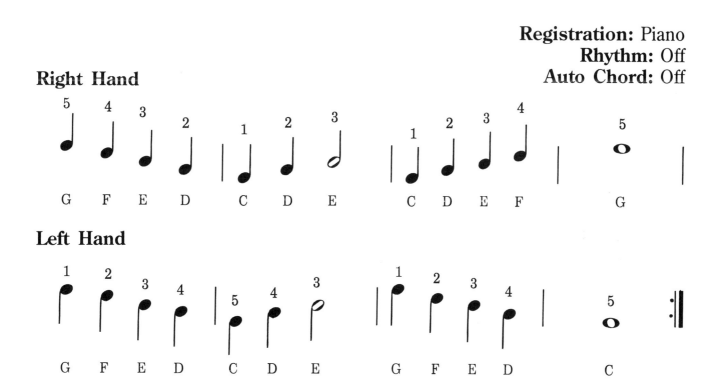

Skipping on the Keyboard

Music doesn't always *step* from one note to the next. Sometimes it *skips* a letter.

The rule is: skip a note, skip a finger.

CIRCLE the skips in these two songs. Then go back and PLAY the songs.

Registration: Flute
Rhythm: Off
Auto Chord: Off

Right Hand

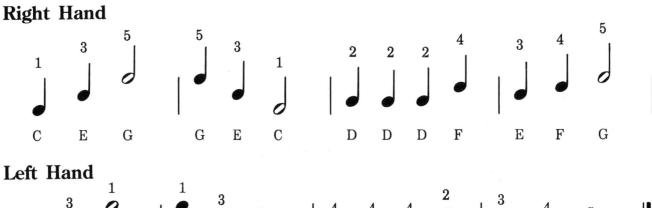

C E G   G E C   D D D F   E F G

Left Hand

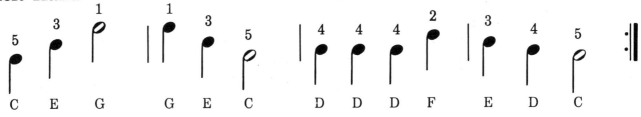

C E G   G E C   D D D F   E D C

Registration: Violin
Rhythm: Off
Auto Chord: Off

Right Hand

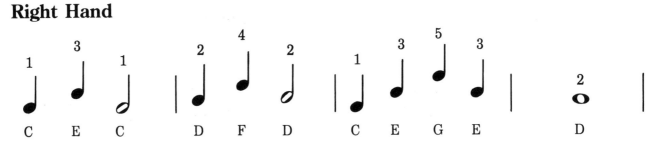

C E C   D F D   C E G E   D

Left Hand

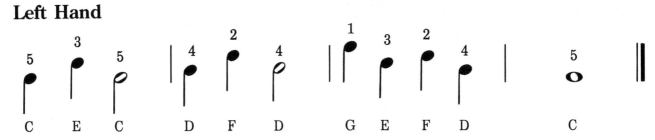

C E C   D F D   G E F D   C

Some notes stay the same, instead of moving up and down. These are called *repeated* notes.

Can you find the repeated notes in these songs?

Jingle Bells

Registration: Music Box
Rhythm: Off
Auto Chord: Off

Right Hand

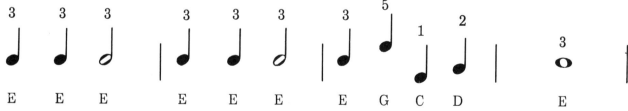

3	3	3	3	3	3	3	5	1	2	3
E	E	E	E	E	E	E	G	C	D	E

Left Hand

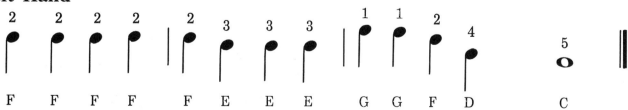

2	2	2	2	2	3	3	3	1	1	2	4	5
F	F	F	F	F	E	E	E	G	G	F	D	C

Love Somebody

Registration: Piano
Rhythm: Off
Auto Chord: Off

Right Hand

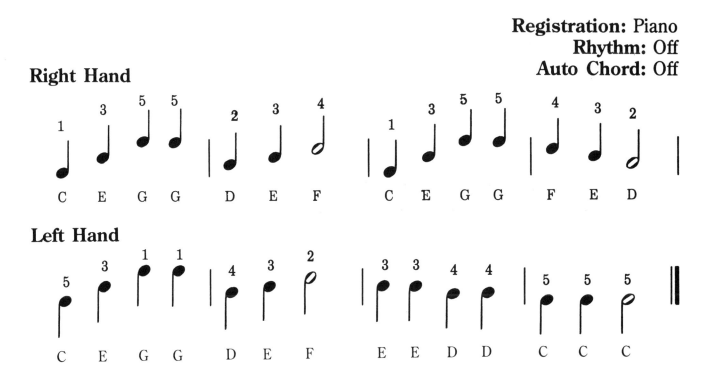

| C | E | G | G | D | E | F | C | E | G | G | F | E | D |

Left Hand

| C | E | G | G | D | E | F | E | E | D | D | C | C | C |

The Grand Staff

We put music notes on *lines* and *spaces* to make it easier to see how they move. These five lines and four spaces make a *staff*

Lines   **Spaces**

Two *staves* can be used–one for the right hand, and one for the left hand. The *treble clef* is usually used to mark the staff played by your right hand. The *bass clef* is used to mark the staff played by your left hand.

Treble Clef
(also known as the G Clef)

Bass Clef
(also known as the F Clef)

Treble Staff   **Bass Staff**

When we play with both hands together, the two staves are connected by a *brace.* This is called the *grand staff.*

Brace ——————→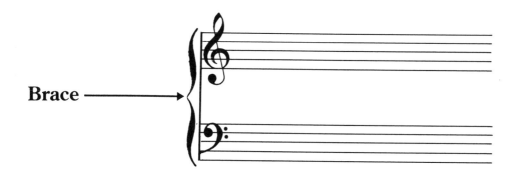

This is how notes look on the lines and spaces of the staff.

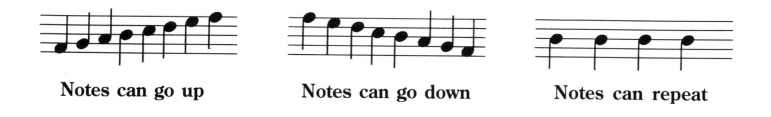

Notes can go up   **Notes can go down**   **Notes can repeat**

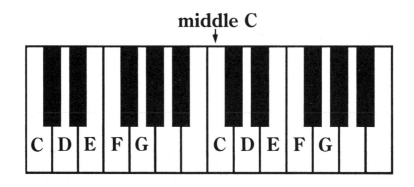

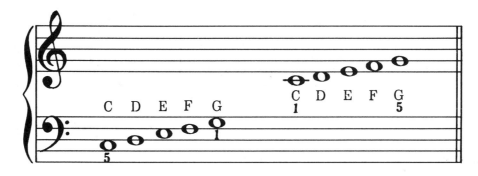

PLACE both hands on the keyboard, as shown above.

KEEP your fingers curved.
WATCH your music–not your hands.

PRACTICE playing the notes on the staff above.
SAY each note name as you PLAY it.

Now you're ready for your first song on a staff.

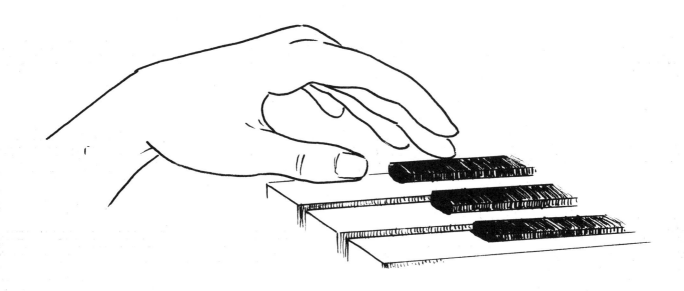

Reading Staff Notes!

Registration: Piano
Rhythm: Off
Auto Chord: Off

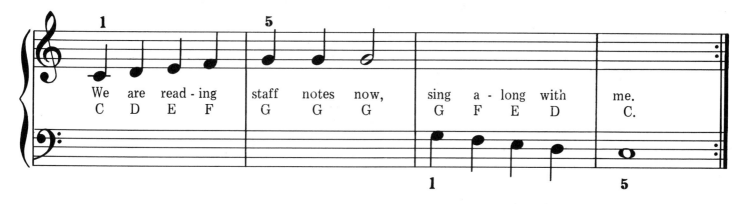

More Staff Notes!

Registration: Piano
Rhythm: Off
Auto Chord: Off

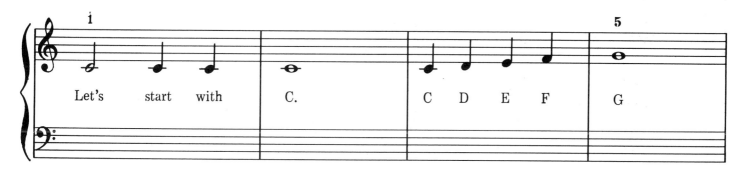

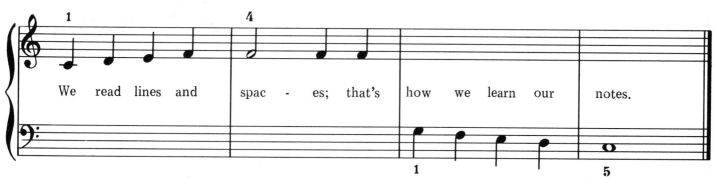

Rhythm Review

Music has long sounds and short sounds. When we put them together, we call this *rhythm*.

We have been counting rhythm by saying "quarter," "half-note," or "great-big-whole-note."

Now let's feel the rhythm by counting with numbers.

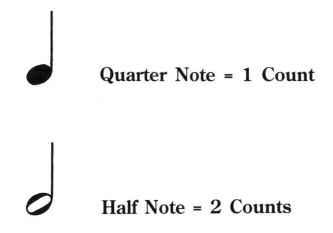

Quarter Note = 1 Count

Half Note = 2 Counts

Whole Note = 4 Counts

In your first song, you counted like this:

quarter   quarter   half-note   half-note   half-note

Now let's count with numbers:

Count: 1   2   3 4   1   2   3 4   1   2   3 4   1   2   3 4

NOTICE that every measure has the same amount of beats. Each measure begins with a count of 1.

Learning About Time Signatures

We show the number of counts in a measure with a *time signature*. The time signature is the two numbers at the beginning of each song.

The *top number* tells *how many* counts or beats are in each measure.

The *bottom number* tells *what kind* of note gets one count or beat.

Here is a time signature.

4 ←———— **Four beats in every measure.**
4 ←———— **The quarter note gets one beat.**

We have already learned the song "Reading Staff Notes." Now let's PLAY it again, COUNTING aloud this time.

Reading Staff Notes!

Registration: Piano
Rhythm: Off
Auto Chord: Off

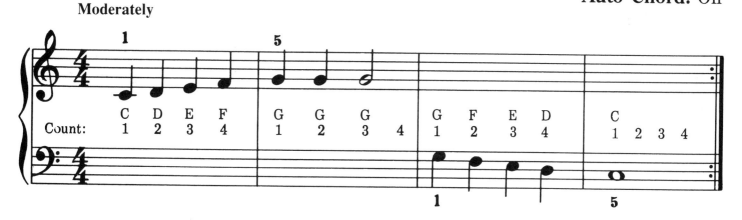

Hot Cross Buns

Registration: Organ
Rhythm: Off
Auto Chord: Off

Moderately

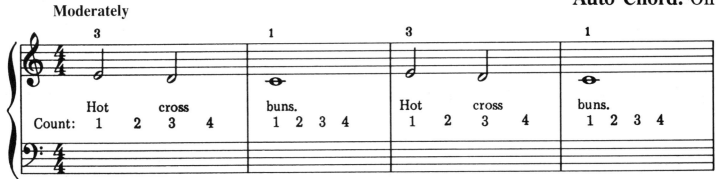

Count:	Hot	cross	buns.	Hot	cross	buns.
	1 2 3 4		1 2 3 4	1 2 3 4		1 2 3 4

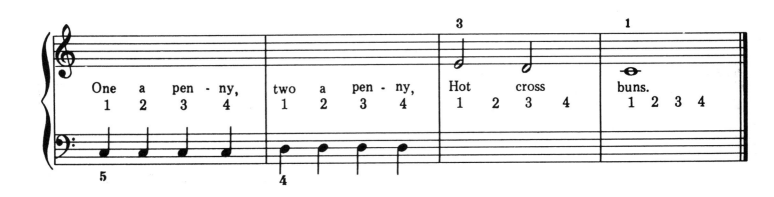

One	a	pen - ny,	two	a	pen - ny,	Hot	cross	buns.
1 2 3 4			1 2 3 4			1 2 3 4		1 2 3 4

Here is another time signature.

2 ◄——————— **Two beats in every measure.**
4 ◄——————— **The quarter note gets one beat.**

PLAY this next song and COUNT the rhythm.
Now PLAY it again and SING the words as you play.

Birdies in the Trees

Registration: Flute
Rhythm: Off
Auto Chord: Off

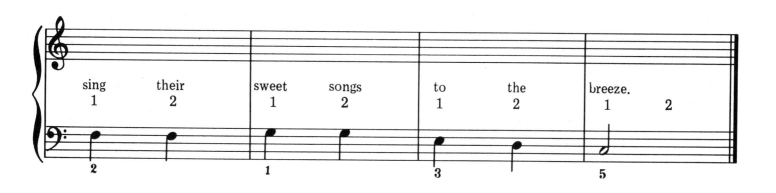

The Dotted Half Note

The *dotted half note* is worth three beats. It looks like this:

Dotted Half Note

Here is a rule that makes the dotted half note easy to remember: Count 2 beats for the half note; 1 beat for the dot. That makes 3 beats for the dotted half note.

Here is another time signature. $\frac{3}{4}$

3 ◄——Three beats in every measure.
4 ◄——The quarter note gets one beat.

Remember, the top number tells how many beats are in each measure. The bottom number tells what kind of note gets one beat.

When notes are piled up on top of one another on the staff, they should be played together. In the next song, practice each hand alone, then put both hands together.

SAY the note names as you play.
Be sure to COUNT the rhythm silently to yourself.

Lazy Mary

Registration: Piano
Rhythm: Off
Auto Chord: Off

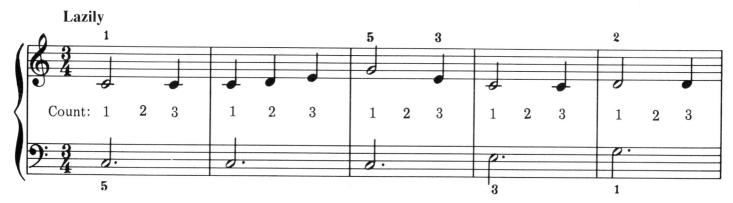

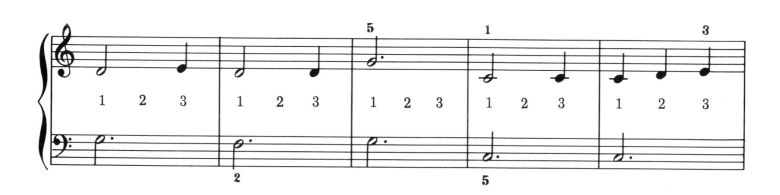

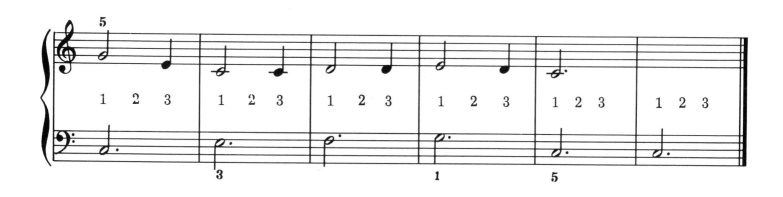

Rests

Rests are places where your hands don't play. Rests have the same names and the same values as the kinds of notes you have learned.

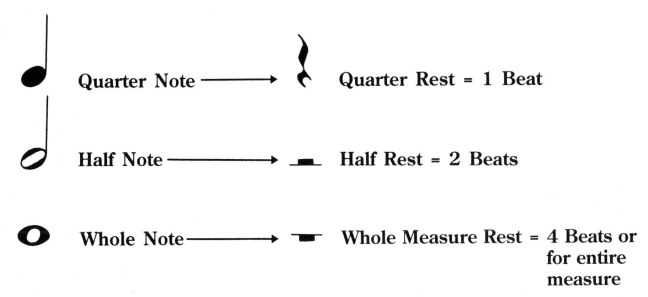

Quarter Note ⟶ Quarter Rest = 1 Beat

Half Note ⟶ Half Rest = 2 Beats

Whole Note ⟶ Whole Measure Rest = 4 Beats or for entire measure

As you play "The Resting Song," LIFT your hands slightly off the keys for the rests, and count out the rhythm of the rest in a whisper.

The Resting Song

Registration: Piano
Rhythm: Off
Auto Chord: Off

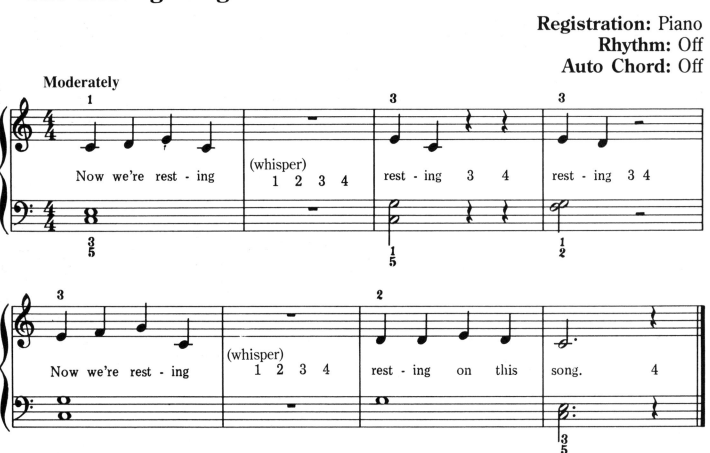

LEARN each hand of this next song separately before putting both hands together.

Sleep, Baby, Sleep

Registration: Organ
Rhythm: Off
Auto Chord: Off

Moderately slow

Sleep, ba - by, sleep. Thy fa - ther guards the sheep. Thy

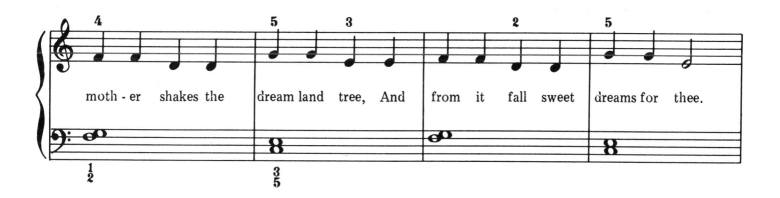

moth - er shakes the dream land tree, And from it fall sweet dreams for thee.

Sleep, ba - by, sleep. Sleep, ba - by, sleep.

Broken Measures

If the very first measure of a song does not have as many beats as the time signature says it should, then this is a *broken,* or *incomplete measure.* Part of the measure is at the beginning of the song, and the other part is at the end. Together the two parts add up to the time signature's top number. We call the notes in the first part of the broken measure *pickup notes.*

PLAY this next song and COUNT the rhythm aloud. NOTICE the song begins with a count of 3.

Poor Broken Measures

Registration: Piano
Rhythm: Off
Auto Chord: Off

Auto Rhythm

Your keyboard can make different rhythms that you can use while you are playing songs. When you use these rhythms, it is like playing with a drummer in a band.

First turn on the *Rhythm* section. Then find the rhythm that is chosen for you in the guide at the beginning of each song. Now adjust the *Tempo* control to find a speed that is not too fast or slow for you. Most keyboards have a light that flashes, either every beat or on the first beat of each measure. Not only will you be able to hear the beats, but you will be able to see them too!

Let's add our *Rhythm* section to this next song. PLAY slowly so the notes and the rhythm go together smoothly.

A Very Smart Song

Registration: Piano
Rhythm: Swing
Auto Chord: Off

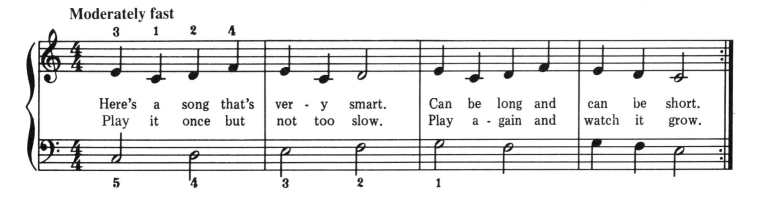

Now PLAY the next song with a *waltz* rhythm.

Here at the Circus

Registration: Organ
Rhythm: Waltz
Auto Chord: Off

Moderately

Here we are at the cir - cus, We
love to go to the cir - cus, We
see clowns here at the cir - cus, And
mon - keys and li - ons and more. Oh boy!

Now PLAY the next song with a *swing* rhythm.

A Happy Song

Registration: Piano
Rhythm: Swing
Auto Chord: Off

Ties

A *tie* is a curved line that connects two notes on the same line or space. PLAY the first note only and HOLD it down while you COUNT both notes.

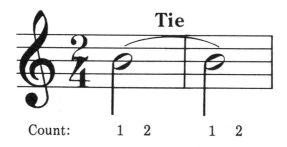

All Tied Up!

Registration: Violin
Rhythm: Off
Auto Chord: Off

Now PLAY the song again and add a *swing* rhythm.

Single Finger Chords

A *chord* is three or more notes that sound good when you put them together. Even though chords can be played with either the right or left hand, we usually play them with the left hand to go with the melody in the right hand.

It usually takes three fingers to play a three-note chord, but we can play a chord with just one finger by using the *Single Finger* control in your *Auto Chord* section. This is the lowest part of your keyboard.

Most keyboards have two different controls for playing chords–*Single Finger,* and *Fingered.* To play single finger chords, turn on the control that is marked *Single Finger,* or *On.* The letter names of the notes are written above the *Auto Chord* section. These are the only notes that can be used with the *Single Finger* or *Fingered* controls on your keyboard.

When you want to play a single finger chord, just play the note that names the chord. The names of the chords are always written above the notes.

For example, if you want to play a C chord, press down the C note in the Auto Chord section with the second finger of your left hand. If you want to play a G chord, press down the G note the same way. You must hold the key down until the chord changes or the chord will stop playing.

One, Two

Registration: Piano
Rhythm: Off
Auto Chord: Single Finger

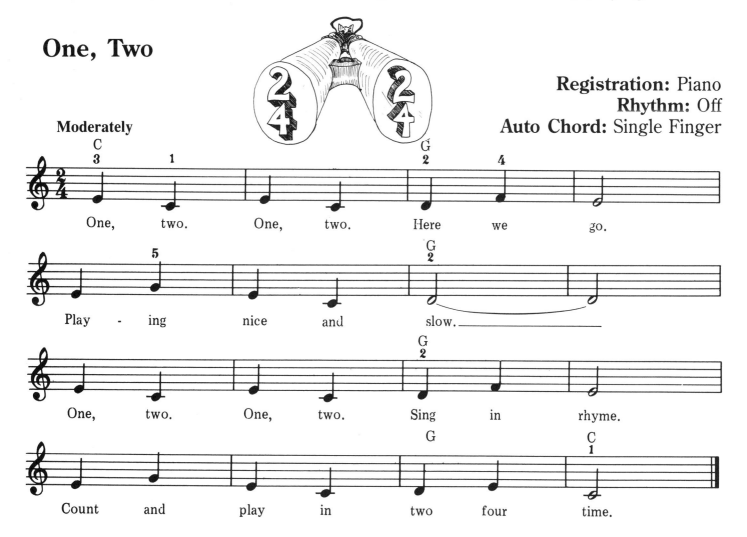

Now let's add the *Rhythm* section. When you do this, the chords will practically play themselves! Just press down the key for the chord you want, and let go. Your keyboard will keep playing that chord until you change chords. Some keyboards have a *Memory* button. If yours does, just press this down along with your *Single Finger* control to keep the chords playing by themselves.

Go Tell Aunt Rhody

Registration: Piano
Rhythm: Swing
Auto Chord: Single Finger

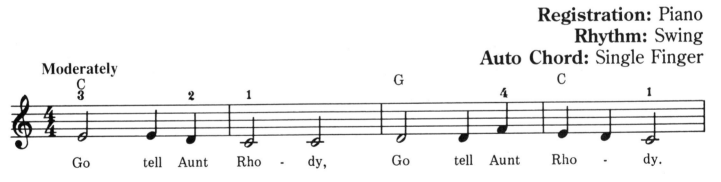

Go tell Aunt Rho - dy, Go tell Aunt Rho - dy.

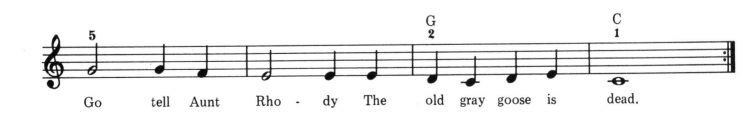

Go tell Aunt Rho - dy The old gray goose is dead.

Synchro Start

Most keyboards have a *Synchro Start* control. When you use it, the rhythm will start as soon as you play a note in the *Auto Chord* section of your keyboard.

To use Synchro Start, first turn on your *Rhythm* section to find the rhythm and speed you want to play. When you are ready, turn the rhythm off and turn Synchro Start on. On most keyboards, the rhythm will flash the tempo for you silently until you are ready to play.

Waltz Time

Registration: Violin
Rhythm: Waltz
Auto Chord: Single Finger

Here I am play - ing in waltz time.

Sing - ing and count - ing to three.

Play - ing my key - board in waltz time.

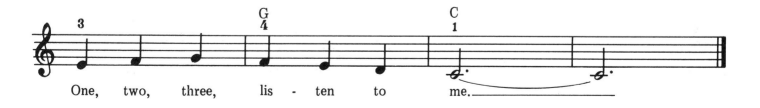

One, two, three, lis - ten to me.

Dynamics

Dynamics are signs that tell how loud or soft music should be played. If your keyboard is *touch-sensitive,* you will be able to play your songs using dynamics.

Touch-sensitive, means that you can play loud or soft, depending on how hard you strike the keys. If the keyboard is not touch-sensitive, you must adjust the volume to how loud or soft you want before you play. Here's a list of the most common dynamic markings, their names, and what they mean.

pp	=	pianissimo	=	very soft
p	=	piano	=	soft
mp	=	mezzo piano	=	medium soft
mf	=	mezzo forte	=	medium loud
f	=	forte	=	loud
ff	=	fortissimo	=	very loud

Let's PLAY this next song using *dynamics.* PRACTICE each hand alone first, then put both hands together. The dynamic marking *ff* means you should play the song very loudly all the way through.

Playing in a Marching Band

Registration: Trumpet
Rhythm: Off
Auto Chord: Off

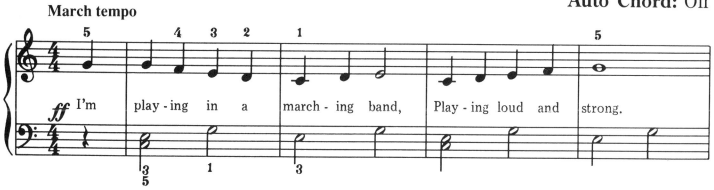

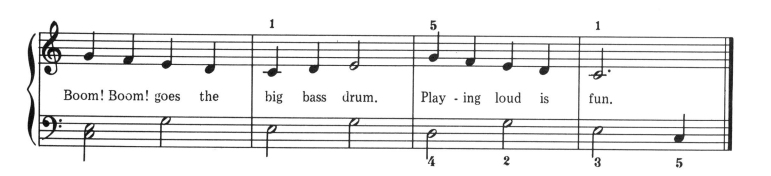

This next song has the dynamic marking *pp* at the beginning.
PLAY this song all the way through very softly.

Somebody's Sleeping

Registration: Organ
Rhythm: Off
Auto Chord: Off

This next song uses the *f* dynamic marking. PLAY it through loud and strong.

First PRESS Synchro Start.
REMEMBER, the rhythm will start as soon as you play a note in your Auto Chord section, not when you play the pickup notes alone.

My Trumpet

Registration: Trumpet
Rhythm: Swing
Auto Chord: Single Finger

Phrases

A *phrase* is a musical sentence. A curved line called a *slur* or *phrase mark* over or under a group of notes on different lines or spaces makes a *phrase*.

Can you tell the difference between phrases and ties?

Good Morning Song

Registration: Piano
Rhythm: Off
Auto Chord: Off

Be sure to PRACTICE each hand alone before putting both hands together.

Remember to SELECT the right tempo before you PRESS Synchro Start. Be sure to LIFT your hand off the keyboard lightly to make a break at the end of each phrase.

Now PLAY the "German Song."

German Song

Registration: Trombone
Rhythm: Waltz
Auto Chord: Single Finger

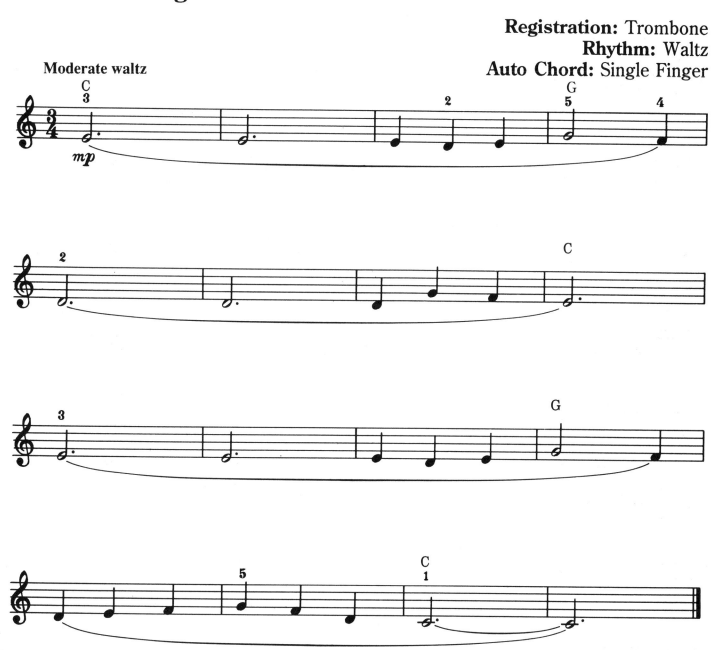

44

New Notes

Sometimes it is necessary to reach your fifth finger over to new notes beyond those you have been using.

POSITION the thumb of your right hand at Middle C.
REACH up with your pinky to A, then to B, then to High C.

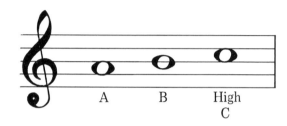

Let's also move the fifth finger of your left hand to the next closest key.

POSITION the thumb of your left hand thumb at G.
REACH down with your pinky to Low B.

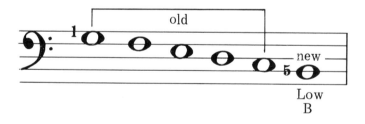

PLAY each of these new notes.
SING their names as you play them.

Reaching Out

Registration: Piano
Rhythm: Off
Auto Chord: Off

I and V7 Chords

You have already learned to play the C and G chords using a single finger. A three-note chord can be built by using three fingers. Once you learn how to build chords, you will be able to play many songs.

Chords have letter names. Chords are also numbered with *Roman numerals.*

C Chord = I (One) Chord

To build a I chord, place the pinky of your left hand on Low C. Now place your middle finger on E and your thumb on G.

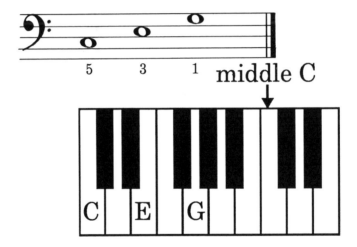

PLAY these notes all at the same time.

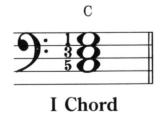

I Chord

We can turn the G chord to a G7 chord by changing one of its notes.

G7 Chord = V7 (Five-Seven) Chord

To make a V7 chord from a I chord, keep the top note the same. Now play the note right next to it with your second finger, and move your pinky down to the very next key.

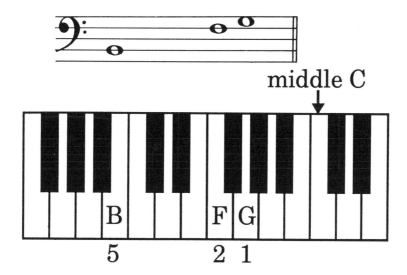

PLAY these three notes at the same time.

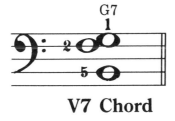

V7 Chord

PRACTICE changing from the I chord to the V7 chord. LOOK only at the music–not at your hand.

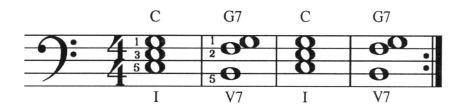

48

Now PLAY the next two songs.

Ode to Joy

Registration: Trumpet
Rhythm: Off
Auto Chord: Off

Ludwig van Beethoven (1770–1827)

Lightly Row

Registration: Piano
Rhythm: Off
Auto Chord: Off

Single Finger G7 Chords

You have already learned how to form a G7 chord. Now let's learn how to play G7 chords using our *Single Finger* control. To do this, you need to play other keys besides the G key. You can play G7 chords different ways, depending on the make of your keyboard. Here are some rules to follow.

If you have a Casio keyboard, play a G, then the very next two white keys to the right. This means you will be playing G, A, and B at the same time.

If you have a Yamaha keyboard, play a G, then the very next white key to the left. This means you will be playing F and G at the same time. Other makes of keyboards also follow this rule. Check your owner's manual to be sure.

Now that you know how to form a G7 chord, you can use the same steps to form other V7 chords.

PLAY the next two songs using the single finger C and G7 chords.

Oats, Peas, Beans, and Barley Grow

Registration: Piano
Rhythm: Waltz
Auto Chord: Single Finger

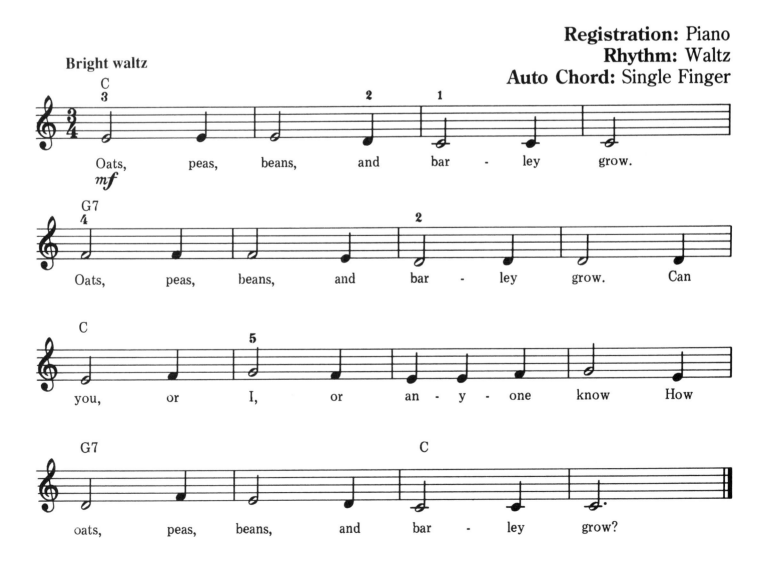

A Tisket a Tasket

Registration: Organ
Rhythm: Swing
Auto Chord: Single Finger

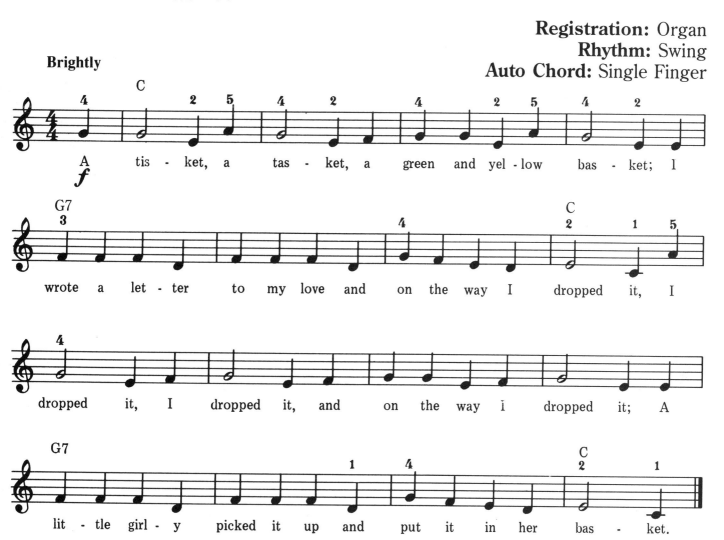

The IV Chord

The more chords you know, the more songs you will be able to play.

F Chord = IV (Four) Chord

To build a IV chord, keep the bottom note the same. MOVE the other two fingers up one letter.

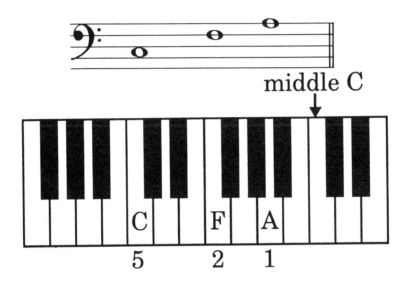

PLAY these three notes all at the same time.

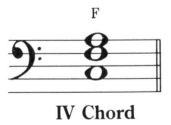

IV Chord

PRACTICE changing from the I chord to the IV chord several times. LOOK only at the music–not at your hand.

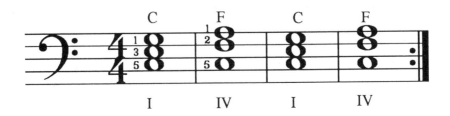

Now let's try the next song.

LEARN each hand alone before putting both hands together. Be careful to use the correct fingering.

Springtime

Registration: Violin
Rhythm: Off
Auto Chord: Off

Play "Springtime" again, this time adding a *waltz* rhythm.

54

Now let's play IV chords using single finger chords.

PRACTICE changing from C to F to G7. Be careful not to strike any other notes, or you will get a different chord than the one that you want.

Now PLAY the next two songs.

Hey Diddle Diddle

Registration: Piano
Rhythm: Waltz
Auto Chord: Single Finger

Moderately fast

Hey did - dle did - dle, the cat and the fid - dle, The

cow jumped o - ver the moon._____ The

lit - tle dog laugh - ed to see such soprt, And the

dish ran a - way with the spoon._____

When the Saints Go Marching In

Registration: Clarinet
Rhythm: Swing
Auto Chord: Single Finger

Bright and lively

Oh, when the saints_____ go march-ing in._____ Oh, when the

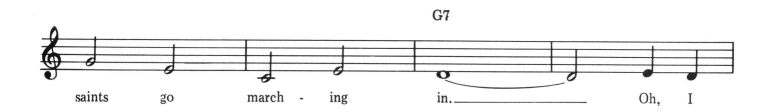

saints go march - ing in._____ Oh, I

want to be in that num - ber,_____ When the

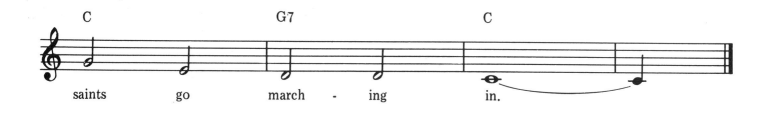

saints go march - ing in.

Eighth Notes

These are two *eighth notes:*

Eighth Notes

One *eighth note* looks like this:

Eighth Note

The *eighth rest* looks like this:

Eighth Rest

Eighth notes are faster than quarter notes. Let's prove it!

 = 1/2 Beat

♪ + ♪ = ♩

1/2 + 1/2 = 1 Beat

USE the word "and" to count notes worth 1/2 beat.
SAY and CLAP the following rhythm.

$\frac{4}{4}$ 1 and 2 and 3   4   1 and 2 and 3 4   1 and 2 and 3 4 and   1   2   3   4

LEARN each hand of this next song separately.
COUNT aloud as you play.

Country Dance

Registration: Organ
Rhythm: Off
Auto Chord: Off

PLAY "Country Dance" again, and add a *swing* rhythm to it.

PLAY this next song without the Rhythm section. Practice slowly to get the eighth notes even. When you are ready to add the Rhythm section, SET the tempo, then PRESS Synchro Start and begin.

Oh, Susannah

Registration: Piano
Rhythm: Swing
Auto Chord: Single Finger
Stephen Foster (1826-1864)

Oh, I come from Al - a - bam - a with my ban - jo on my knee, And I'm

goin' to Lou' - si - an - a for my true love for to see.

Oh, Su - san - nah, oh, don't you cry for me, For I'm

gone to Lou' - si - an - a with my ban - jo on my knee.

Middle C Position

Here is a new position to play.

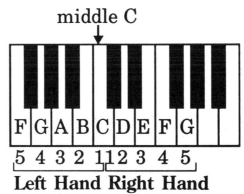

PLACE both hands on your keyboard as shown in the picture above.
PLAY each note and SAY its letter name aloud.

Now try this next song.

Changing Places

Registration: Piano
Rhythm: Off
Auto Chord: Off

Sharps

A *sharp sign* (♯) next to a note means to play the very next note to the right. Sharps go up. They make a note sound higher.

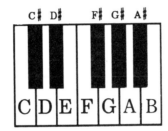

Using your second finger, PLAY each white key and then its sharp.
SAY the names of the notes as you play them.
Do the sharped notes sound higher to you?
Which two notes do not have black sharps?

PLAY the next two songs.

Sharps on the Move

Moderately fast

Registration: Piano
Rhythm: Off
Auto Chord: Off

Swanee River

Registration: Organ
Rhythm: Off
Auto Chord: Off
Stephen Foster (1826-1864)

Now PLAY "Swanee River" again with a *swing* rhythm.

Flats

A flat sign (♭) next to a note means to play the very next closest note to the left. Flats go down. They make a note sound lower.

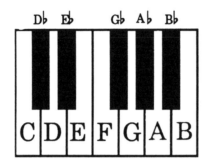

Using your second finger, PLAY each white key and then its flat. SAY the names of the notes as you play them.

Do the flatted notes sound lower to you?
Which two notes do not have black flats?

Flats for Sale!

Registration: Piano
Rhythm: Off
Auto Chord: Off

also B♭ because it's
in the same measure

Introducing G Position

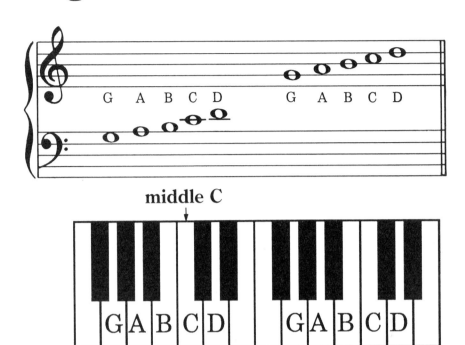

middle C

PLACE both hands on your keyboard in the G position, as shown in the picture above.

PLAY each note and SAY its letter name aloud.

PLACE both hands in the G position.

SAY each note's name aloud as you PLAY this song.

Playing in G

Registration: Piano
Rhythm: Off
Auto Chord: Off

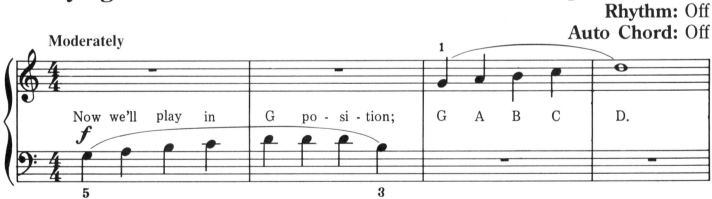

Now we'll play in / G po - si - tion; / G A B C / D.

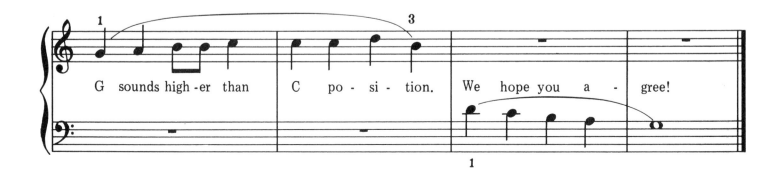

G sounds high - er than / C po - si - tion. / We hope you a - / gree!

The G Position I, IV, and V7 Chords

The G position chords are built in the same way as the C position chords. They also use the same fingering.

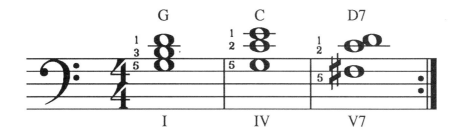

PRACTICE changing from chord to chord, without looking at your hand.

REVIEW the C position chords, using the same fingers as for the G position chords.

Jump for Joy

Registration: Flute
Rhythm: Off
Auto Chord: Off

Play "Jump for Joy" again, this time adding a *swing* rhythm.

Polly Wolly Doodle

Registration: Guitar
Rhythm: Off
Auto Chord: Off

Moderately fast

also F♯ because it's in the same measure

PLAY "Polly Wolly Doodle" once more. This time ADD a *country* or *swing* rhythm.

Now let's play the G position chords using single finger chords. We
have already played songs using C and G chords. To make a single finger
D7 Chord, just follow the same rules for forming a G7 chord, starting on a
D instead of a G.

Look at Me!

Registration: Flute
Rhythm: Swing
Auto Chord: Single Finger

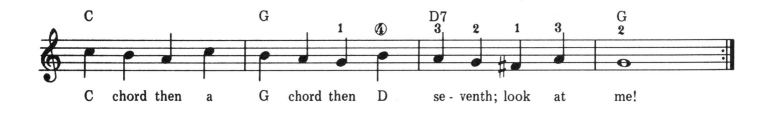

Fingered Chords

We have already learned how to add accompaniment to our one-finger chords by using the *Single Finger* chord setting in the Auto Chord section of our keyboard. We can also add accompaniment to our three-note chords by using the *Fingered* chord setting in the Auto Chord section.

When you do this, you can only use keys in the Auto Chord section to form your fingered chords, and so you will have to play your chords in the lower part of your keyboard. To do this, just move your left hand one *octave* (eight notes) lower, so that it is within the marked range of the Auto Chord section. Now play your chords the same way you did before. Since fingered chords are played in the lower part of the keyboard, they sound lower and are also written lower on the bass staff.

This is how G position chords played in the Auto Chord section will be written.

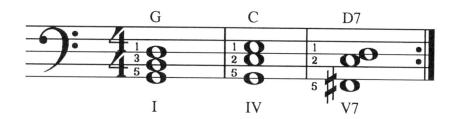

PRACTICE changing from chord to chord in this *low G position* without looking at your hands.

Remember, fingered chords work and sound the same as single finger chords, except that you build them all by yourself. After you play each chord, let go, and get ready to play the next chord. We use ties to connect the chords in the bass clef to show that the sound of the chord lasts from measure to measure. You do not need to hold down the chord for the total number of beats of the tied notes. A chord will keep playing by itself until you change to the next chord.

PLAY these next two songs using the *Fingered* chord setting.

Dreaming

Registration: Violin
Rhythm: Waltz
Auto Chord: Fingered

Beautiful Brown Eyes

Registration: Guitar or Piano
Rhythm: Waltz
Auto Chord: Fingered

Introducing F Position

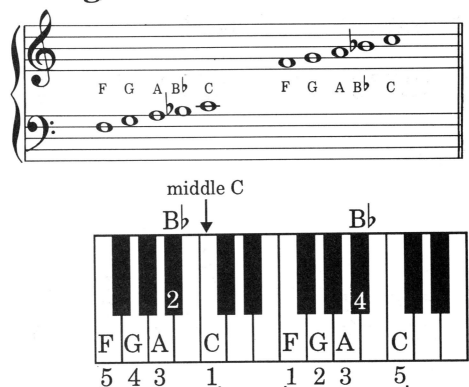

PLACE both hands on your keyboard in the new position shown in the picture above.

PLAY each note and SAY its letter name aloud.

Now PLAY "Exercise in F."

Exercise in F

Registration: Piano
Rhythm: Off
Auto Chord: Off

Moderately

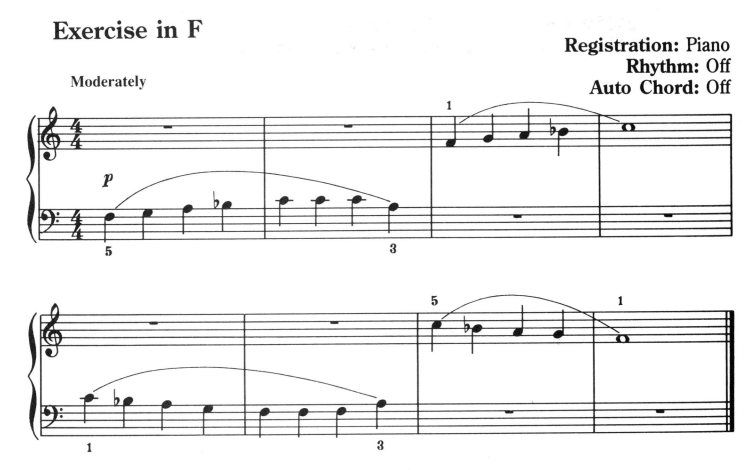

The F Position I, IV, and V7 Chords

The F position chords are built in the same way as the C and G position chords you've already learned. The F position chords also use the same fingering.

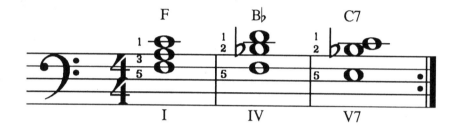

PRACTICE changing from chord to chord, without looking at your hand.

REVIEW the C and G position chords.

PLAY the F, C, and G position chords, using the same fingering.

74

PRACTICE this slowly without the rhythm to get the chord changes even. Then ADD the rhythm.

Skip to My Lou

Clementine

Registration: Guitar
Rhythm: Waltz
Auto Chord: Off

Now let's use fingered chords for this next song. Remember, you will need to play your chords one octave lower, in low F position, when you use the Fingered Chord setting in the Auto Chord section. Practice the left-hand part by itself before adding the right-hand part.

This Old Man

Registration: Piano
Rhythm: March or Swing
Auto Chord: Fingered

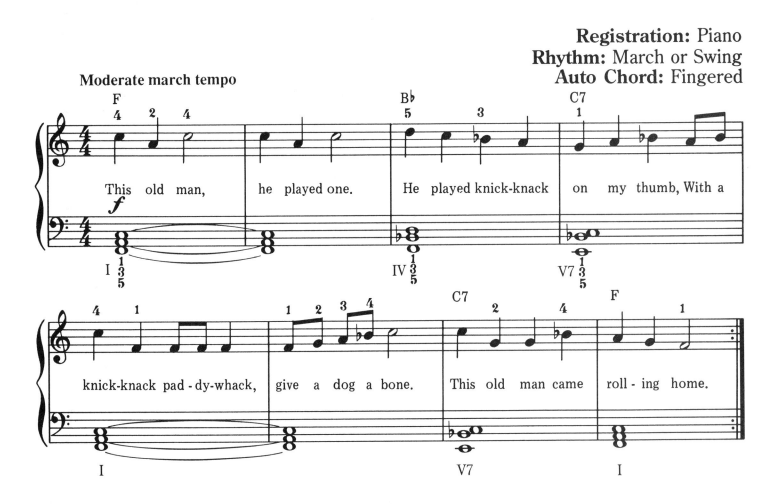

Fill-Ins

Many keyboards have a *fill-in* button. When you press this, the Rhythm section will play a one-measure drum solo.

As you PLAY the next song, press down with your left hand at the beginning of the measures marked *Fill-In.* COUNT the beats carefully so you will be ready to continue your song after the fill-in.

If your keyboard doesn't have a Fill-In button, just play the song straight through. Take care to observe the measures of rest where the fill-in would occur.

Polka

Registration: Organ
Rhythm: Polka or Swing
Auto Chord: Single Finger

Variations

Some keyboards have a *Variation* button or control. The Variation button adds a fancy background when you play your song. Let's try using it with this next song. Don't let the background confuse you. If you don't have a Variation button, just play the song as written.

Barcarolle

Registration: Vibraphone
Rhythm: Waltz
Auto Chord: Fingered

WORNSTAFF MEMORIAL LIBRARY
ASHLEY, OHIO 43003